PO**R/

LET**NG

ACKNOWLEDGEMENT

The authors, Carolyn Davis and Charlene Brown, would like to thank all of the following for their patience and support: Sally Black, Sally Marshall Corngold, Pat Brown and our friends at Marian Bergeson Elementary and of course, the wonderful staff at Walter Foster Publishing.

INTRODUCTION

Making posters and signs is fun, and useful, too! You may need to advertise your thirst quenching lemonade, a garage sale or a school election. Or, perhaps you just enjoy the art world and would like to improve your lettering and design skills. Whatever the reason, we are going to show you how to make posters and cards for school, business, community and for fun!

Signs and posters are easy to make. Before you begin, choose the size, color and style you want to use. You can get ideas by looking at books, magazines, signs and posters. Notice the designs, color arrangements, letter styles and sizes.

Signs and posters can be even more fun when you add a picture or drawing (you may want to refer to our book, "Drawing Fun" for techniques).

Just for fun, in chapter four we will show you how to make creative games. We will make a store, a birthday party and a restaurant.

You can copy our ideas or make up your own. Just remember—use your imagination and HAVE FUN!

GLOSSARY

COLLAGE—An art form in which various parts of objects, drawings and pictures are arranged to make one poster or art piece.

DESIGN OR LAYOUT—The arrangement of the parts of your poster. You want to plan the arrangement of the lettering, pictures and drawings before you actually paste or draw them on your poster board.

DETAILS—A small part of the whole picture such as curliques, bows, other decorations, photos, or drawings, et cetera.

LETTERING STYLES—Different designs and sizes of letters. Examples of lettering styles are: script, block, italic, outline, bold and fancy. Some styles combine designs such as "bold block."

MEDIUMS—Various materials used to create art. Watercolor paints, oil paints, pen and pencil are all different mediums.

PARALLEL LINES—Two or more straight lines that run even with each other. The rails of a railroad track are parallel to each other. In lettering, you use parallel lines to help you make your letters straight.

SERIF—The small lines or strokes at the tops or bottoms of certain lettering styles. Serif letter example: A. Non Serif (or "Sans Serif") letter example: A.

STENCIL—A plastic template that has the alphabet, numbers or other designs cut out of it.

CONTENTS

MATERIALS

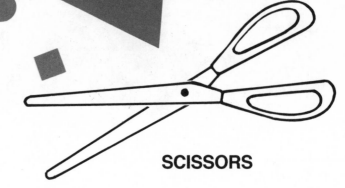

SCISSORS

POSTER BOARD

RULER

The ruler is used for measuring and drawing straight lines.

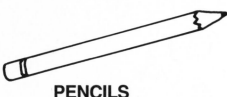

PENCILS

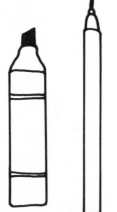

PRESS ON LETTERS

FELT TIP PENS

Felt tip pens come in many bright colors. They can have fine tips or very wide tips, and water base or permanent ink. They are also called marking pens or art markers. You can buy them one at a time or in packages.

GLITTER PAINT

6.

MATERIALS

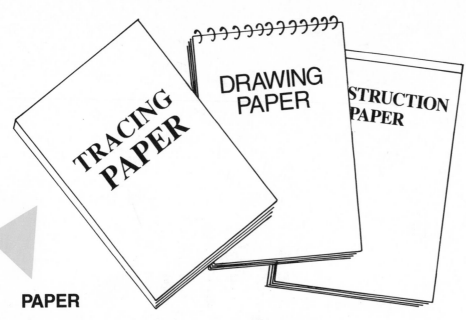

PAPER

You will need construction paper, which comes in many colors and sizes, white drawing paper, and tracing paper.

WHITE GLUE

ERASER

TEMPLATES

STENCILS

POSTER PAINT

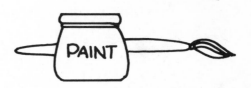

PAINT BRUSH

8.

1.

LETTERING

Lettering can be fun. In this chapter we will learn to make a variety of lettering styles which can be used to create signs, posters, greeting cards — anything fun! You may want to use fancy or script lettering for special projects like birthday party invitations or anniversary cards. The best place to get ideas for different styles of lettering is in magazines, newspapers, books, or on signs. When you start noticing lettering around you, you will see many fun styles. You can even use your imagination to create your own!

BLOCK LETTERING

Block lettering style is the most commonly used lettering style because it is easy to read.

1. Using light pencil, draw parallel lines about one and one half inches apart.
2. Neatly write the alphabet between the lines in light pencil.

3. Use a felt tip pen to write over the pencil lines you want to keep. Make it as neat as you can.
4. Erase the parallel pencil lines when the ink is dry.

Here is an example of the complete alphabet in block lettering for you to copy.

ABCDEFGHIJKLM
NOPQRSTUVWXYZ
abcdefghijklmnop
qrstuvwxyz
0123456789

Try different sizes of felt tip pens or paint to go over your letters.

THIN FELT TIP PEN

ABCDE

THICK FELT TIP PEN

GHIJK

POSTER PAINT

MNOP

11.

TRY OUTLINE LETTERING

1. Using light pencil, draw parallel lines about one and one half inches apart.
2. Neatly write the alphabet between the lines in light pencil.

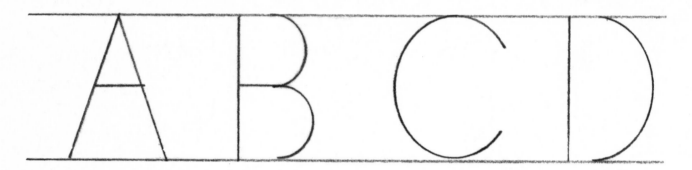

3. Draw an outline around each letter as shown. You can use a ruler or do it freehand.

4. Use a felt tip pen to write over the pencil lines you want to keep. Make it as neat as you can.
5. Erase the parallel pencil lines when the ink is dry.

WRITE YOUR NAME

1. Using light pencil, draw parallel lines about one and one half inches apart.
2. Neatly write your name between the lines in light pencil.

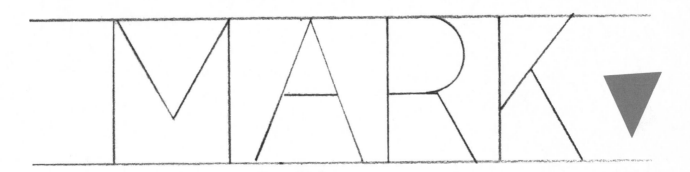

3. Draw an outline around the letters in light pencil, as shown.
4. Use a felt tip pen to draw over the lines you want to keep.

5. Erase the parallel pencil lines when the ink is dry.
6. Color in for fun!

FANCY LETTERS

1. Using light pencil, draw parallel lines about one and one half inches apart.
2. Neatly write the alphabet between the parallel lines with light pencil. Follow the example, or change the shape a little for fun!

Try adding a serif to your letters as shown.

ABCDEFGHIJKLMNO
PQRSTUVWXYZ
abcdefghijklmnopqrs
tuvwxyz
0123456789

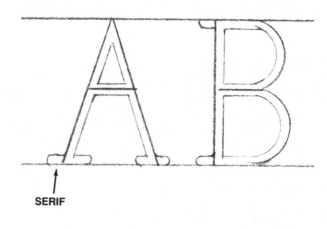

SERIF

Or maybe you would like to try making bold letters.

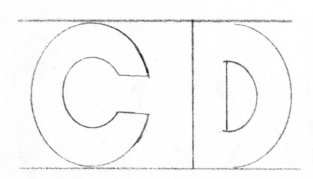

ABCDEFGHIJKLM
NOPQRSTUVWXYZ
abcdefghijklmno
pqrstuvwxyz
0123456789

14.

ABCDEFGHIJKLM
NOPQRSTUVWXYZ
abcdefghijklmno
pqrstuvwxyz
0123456789

Try making the letters a combination of thick and thin.

Try adding a serif to your thick and thin letters.

ABCDEFGHIJKLMNO
PQRSTUVWXYZ
abcdefghijklmnopqrstu
vwxyz
0123456789

Try thick and round.

ABCDEFGHIJKLM
NOPQRSTUVWXYZ
abcdefghijklmnopq
rstuvwxyz
0123456789

Try making your letters wild.

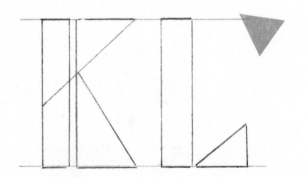

ABCDEFGHIJKLMNOPQ
RSTUVWXYZ
abcdefghijklmnopqrstuv
wxyz
0123456789

15.

ITALICS

Italics are letters that slant upward to the right. To make the angle of your letters consistent, draw in guidelines with pencil that show the angle of each letter, as shown.

ABCDEFGHIJKLM
NOQRSTUVWXYZ
abcdefghijklmnop
qrstuvwxyz
0123456789

Basic Italicized Letters

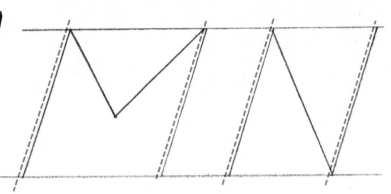

Use your ruler to draw light pencil guidelines.

Italicize your serif thick and thin letters.

ABCDEFGHIJKLMNO
PQRSTUVWXYZ
abcdefghijklmnopqrstu
vwxyz
0123456789

Italicize your thick and round letters.

ABCDEFGHIJKLMNO
PQRSTUVWXYZ
abcdefghijklmnopqrs
tuvwxyz
0123456789

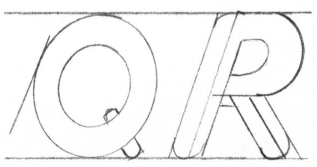

16.

SCRIPT

Script is similar to handwriting. The letters are curved and the lower case letters touch.

1. Using light pencil, draw parallel lines about one and one half inches apart.
2. Neatly write the alphabet between the lines in light pencil.
3. Use a felt tip pen to write over the pencil lines you want to keep. Make it as neat as you can.
4. Erase the parallel pencil lines when the ink is dry.

UPPERCASE SCRIPT LETTERS

LOWERCASE SCRIPT LETTERS

EXAMPLES OF SCRIPT LETTERING:

Rounded Bold Italic Script

ABCDEFGHIJKLM
NOPQRSTUVWXYZ
abcdefghijklmnopqrst
uvwxyz 0123456789

Thick And Thin Script

ABCDEF
GHIJKLMNOP
QRSTUVWXYZ
abcdefghijklmnopqrstuvwxyz
0123456789

STENCILS AND PRESS ON LETTERS

STENCILS

A stencil is a plastic template that has the alphabet, numbers or other designs cut out of it. You use it by laying it down on your paper, then tracing the inside of the letter with your pencil. You can fill the letters in or leave them as they are.

PRESS ON LETTERS

Lay a sheet of letters on your paper or poster board. Use something with a smooth, rounded point—like the end of a ballpoint pen—to gently press or rub over the letter until the letter sticks to the paper. Peel off the sheet of letters. It may take some practice to make the letters stick and look neat.

19.

20.

2.

SIGNS AND POSTERS

Signs and posters are easy to make. Before you begin, choose the size, color and style of lettering you want to use. You can get ideas by looking at books, magazines, signs and posters. Notice the designs, color arrangements, letter styles and sizes.

Signs and posters can be even more fun when you add a picture or drawing. Sign and poster art can be very useful for school and club projects.

SIGNS

1. Plan your project carefully. Decide what the poster or sign should say. Use the least amount of words possible to make it easier to read.
2. Draw a rough layout for your poster on a piece of scrap paper. Decide if you want to add a picture. Try different arrangements and designs.
3. Pick the layout that you like best.

4. Choose the size of letters you will need for the poster. Using a ruler and a pencil, draw parallel lines across your poster, the height of your letters apart. The letters in our example are two inches high for the word "Mike's," and one and one half inches high for the word "Market."

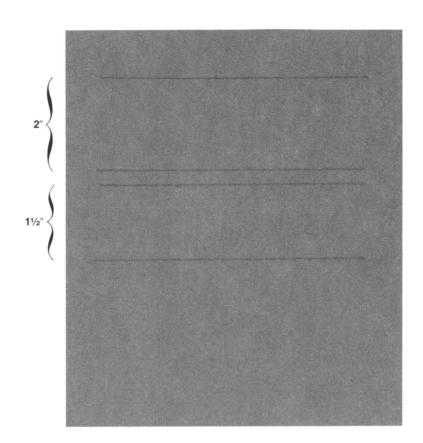

5. To space your letters, draw the middle letter of the word in the center of the parallel lines with light pencil. For example, in the word "Mike's," start with the letter "k."

6. Add the rest of the letters in light pencil, spacing them evenly on either side of the middle letter.

7. Space all of your words this way.

8. Use a felt tip pen to draw over your letters.

9. Erase the parallel pencil lines when the ink is dry.

10. Color the letters if you wish. We have also added a fruit design.

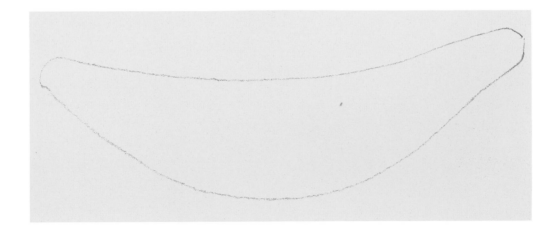

Draw your design or picture on construction paper with pencil, then cut out and glue on your sign.

CENTER

K.

MIKES

CENTER

rk

Market

24.

25.

HAPPY BIRTHDAY POSTER

1. Plan your project carefully. Decide what the poster or sign should say. Use the least amount of words possible to make it easier to read.
2. Draw a rough layout for your poster on a piece of scrap paper. Decide if you want to add a picture. Try different arrangements and designs.
3. Pick the layout that you like best.
4. Choose the size of letters you will need for the poster. Using a ruler and a pencil, draw parallel lines across your poster, the height of your letters apart.
5. To space your letters, draw the middle letter of the word in the center of the parallel lines with light pencil. For example, in the word "Happy," start with the letter "p."
6. Add the rest of the letters in light pencil, spacing them evenly on either side of the middle letter.
7. Space all of your words this way.
8. Use a felt tip pen to draw over your letters.
9. Erase the parallel pencil lines when the ink is dry.

CENTER

10. Color the letters if you wish. We have also added a festive cake and some bright colored pieces of construction paper to make our poster more fun.

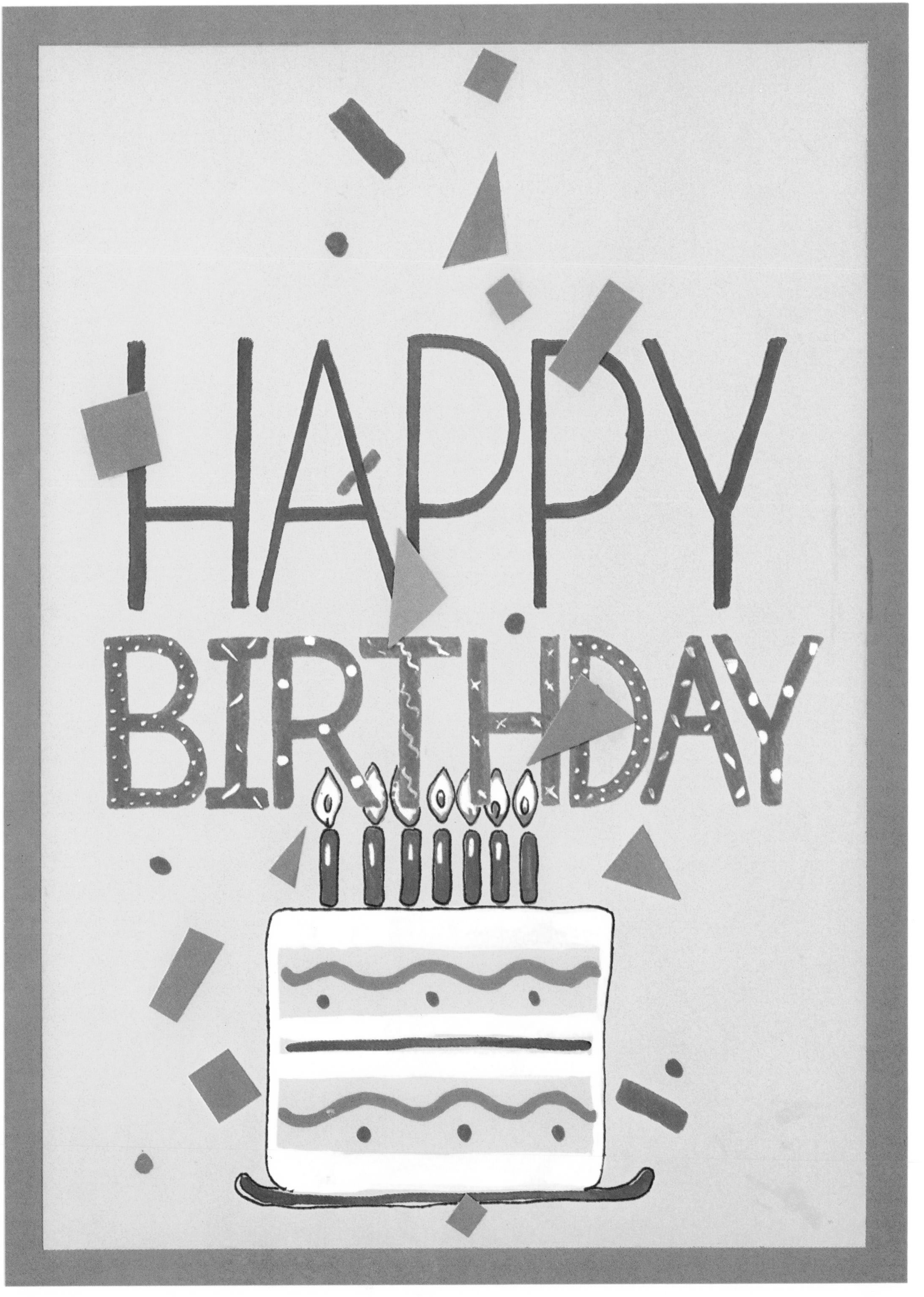
HAPPY
BIRTHDAY

TIFFY'S CAFE

Our sign was made with paint, felt tip pens and some bright colored construction paper.

1. Plan your project carefully. Decide what the poster or sign should say. Use the least amount of words possible to make it easier to read.
2. Draw a rough layout for your poster on a piece of scrap paper. Decide if you want to add a picture. Try different arrangements and designs.
3. Pick the layout that you like best.
4. Choose the size of letters you will need for the poster. Using a ruler and a pencil, draw parallel lines across your poster, the height of your letters apart.

CENTER

5. To space your letters, draw the middle letter of the word in the center of the parallel lines with light pencil.
6. Add the rest of the letters in light pencil, spacing them evenly on either side of the middle letter.
7. Space all of your words this way.
8. Use paint to color your letters.
9. Erase pencil lines when the paint is dry.

28.

Tiffy's CAFE

FRESH LEMONADE

This sign was made of bright construction paper and paint.

1. Plan your project carefully. Decide what the poster or sign should say. Use the least amount of words possible to make it easier to read.
2. Draw a rough layout for your poster on a piece of scrap paper. Decide if you want to add a picture. Try different arrangements and designs.
3. Pick the layout that you like best.
4. The letters for "Lemonade" were cut out of construction paper. The easiest way to do this is to draw the letters on a piece of tissue paper, then color the back of the tissue with pencil (see example). Put the tissue paper on top of your construction paper and trace over the letters. The pencil on the back of the tissue paper will transfer onto the construction paper, just like carbon paper. Now you can cut the letters out.
5. Cut the picture of the cup and the lemons out of construction paper.
6. Glue the pictures and the word "Lemonade" to the sign.
7. Paint the word "Fresh," and the rest of your design on the sign.
8. Erase all pencil lines when the paint is dry.

Color the back of the tissue paper with pencil.

CENTER

CENTER

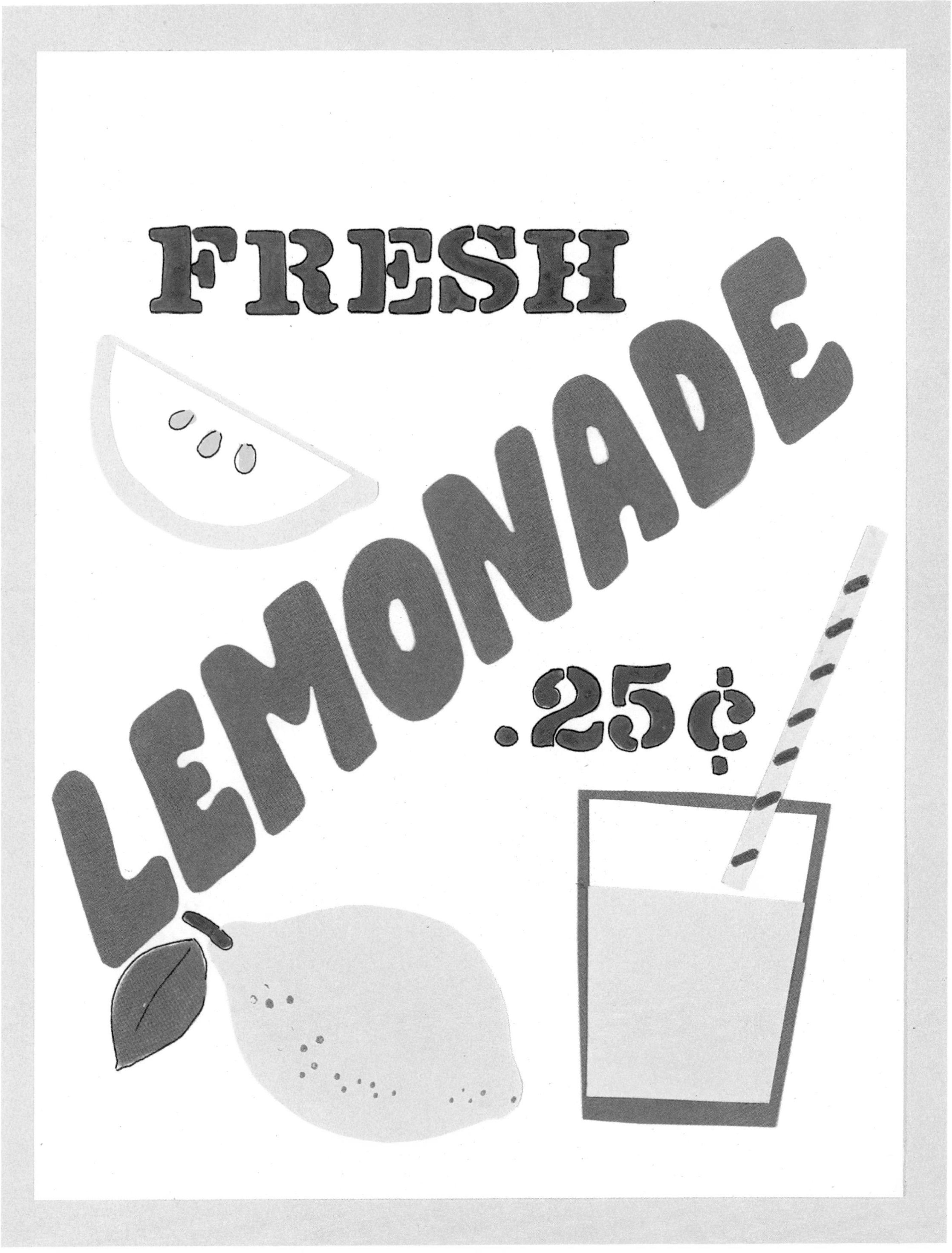
FRESH
LEMONADE
.25¢

HAPPY Holidays

MOTHER

BIRTHDAY PARTY

CARDS

In this chapter we will learn how to use lettering and design to make cards for our family and friends. You can make greeting cards or cards for holidays and special events like Mother's Day, birthdays and anniversaries. There are many ways to make and decorate these cards, and we will show you step by step. You will see how easy it is to personalize a gift or party with hand-made cards and invitations. We hope you will use your imagination and think of many creative ways to use this information.

BIRTHDAY INVITATION

Making an invitation is a lot like making a poster, only smaller. This card was cut out of colorful paper and the lettering was done with felt tip pens.

1. Plan your project carefully. Decide what your card should look like and what it should say. Draw some rough layouts on scrap paper. Try different colors, letter styles and pictures.
2. Pick the layout you like best.

3. Cut the card out of colorful construction paper or white drawing paper, then fold in half.
4. Measure the space for the words on the outside of the card, and draw in light pencil lines. Then, draw each letter carefully, starting with the middle letter.
5. Carefully go over your letters with paint or felt tip pen. Erase pencil lines after the ink or paint is dry.
6. Draw your picture or design on a separate piece of colored paper, then cut out. Use several different colors to make it interesting.
7. Glue the pieces together onto the card.
8. Write all the information about the party on the inside of the card. Write who the party is for, when it will be, what time it starts and where it is. Carefully pencil in the information, then ink over the lines. Erase the pencil lines when the ink is dry.

CHRISTMAS CARD

This card was made by cutting and gluing different colored paper, and lettering with felt tip pens and paint. The word "Happy" was cut out of paper.

1. Plan your project carefully.
2. Cut your card out of construction paper and fold in half.
3. Measure and draw the word "Happy" on a piece of white construction paper in light pencil. Make fat letters. Draw stripes on the letters, then outline in black felt tip pen. Now cut it out.
4. Glue the word "Happy" to your card.

5. Draw the word "Holidays" on your card. We used a script style lettering.

6. Cut holly out of construction paper, then glue onto poster. You can use paint to decorate your card.

7. Erase all pencil lines when ink is dry.

8. Carefully write a message on the inside of your card. Use paint to decorate the inside of your card.

MOTHER'S DAY CARD

This card should be made of heavy drawing paper or watercolor paper so that the front can be painted.

1. Plan your project carefully. Decide what your card should say and what it should look like. Draw some rough sketches on scrap paper. Try different colors, letter styles and pictures.
2. Cut the card out of heavy drawing paper or watercolor paper, then fold in half. We also cut out a heart to glue on our card.
3. On the outside of the card, measure the space for the word or words, then draw in light pencil lines. Draw each letter carefully, beginning with the middle letter. Measure and draw the word "Mother" on the white paper heart with pencil.
4. Glue the paper heart onto your card. Paint the word "Mother" and the flowers and designs on your card.
5. Write a special message to your mother on the inside of the card. We used press on letters for our example.

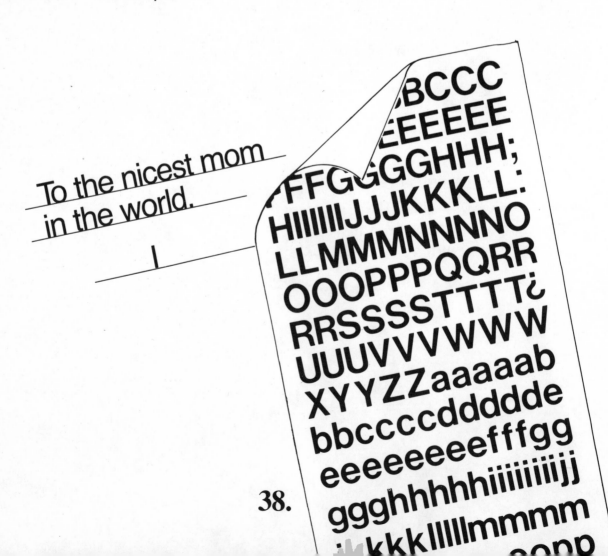

To the nicest mom in the world.

I

38.

To the nicest mom
in the world.

I love you!

Kim

BAKERY

4.

GAMES TO MAKE

In this chapter we will show you how to set up a store, a restaurant and a birthday party. We will make play money, signs, price tags, menus, party hats and place mats that you can play with. You will have as much fun making the pieces for your games as you will playing them. Follow the examples we show you, or use your imagination to make up your own games and parties.

A STORE

Think of all the things you need for a store. Make a list.

1. Money—Dollars and Coins
2. Price Tags
3. Department Signs
4. Receipts
5. Cards For Special Sales

MONEY

COINS—We used yellow construction paper for our coins. Use a round stencil, template or trace real coins to draw different size circles on your paper, then draw the value amount on them. Cut the coins out.

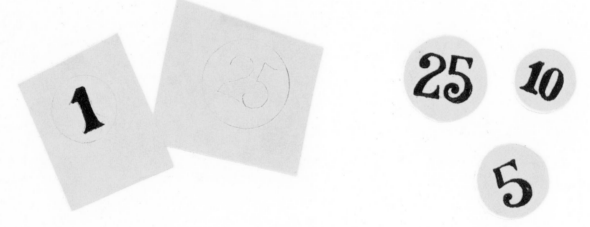

DOLLARS—We used green construction paper for our dollars. Cut some rectangles out of construction paper. Make $1.00, $5.00 And $10.00 Bills. Draw a design and the amount on each bill. You can make the design any way you want, it's your money, but you might want to look at real money for ideas.

PRICE TAGS

The price tags can have the name of the store and the price on them. Cut them out of construction paper, then draw the name of the store and the amount with felt tip pen. Punch a hole in the end for a tie. Add decorations if you like. You can use these over and over again.

DEPARTMENT SIGNS

These signs are for the special departments in your store like vegetables, deli, bakery, toys, and clothes. They can be made with felt tip pens, construction paper and paint. Follow the instructions in the previous chapters. You might want to draw an illustration or cut out a picture from a magazine.

RECEIPTS

Cut out square pieces of paper, all the same size. Using felt tip pen, write the name of your store at the top of each piece, and the word "Total" at the bottom of each piece. Stack the pieces of paper on top of each other with the name at the top. Using rubber cement, glue the top edge of the stack of paper, as shown. (You may have to glue the edge several times.)

GLUE

MIKE'S Market

TOTAL _____

SALE CARDS

These are like small signs. You can make them with construction paper and felt tip pens. Follow the instructions in the previous chapters for lettering, spacing and design.

A RESTAURANT

Make a list of everything you need for a restaurant.

1. Sign
2. Menus
3. Order Pads
4. Money
5. Place Mats

SIGN

Decide what you want the name of your restaurant to be. Decide what colors and letter styles you want to use. Use construction paper, felt tip pens and paint to make your sign. See the example on page 29.

MENU

Choose a bright color of construction paper or drawing paper. Draw the name of your restaurant at the top in light pencil. Using light pencil, draw in the lines where you want to write in the different foods available. Neatly write in the names of the foods and their prices with light pencil. Paint or ink over the light pencil lines. When dry, erase the pencil lines. Decorate your menu with construction paper, paint or felt tip pens.

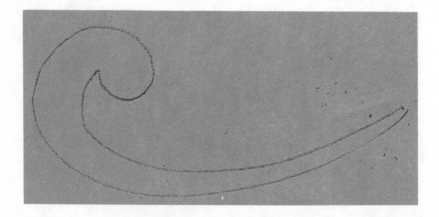

Draw your design on construction paper with light pencil. Cut out the design and glue it on your sign, menu or place mat.

BREAKFAST

EGGS	1.00
TOAST	.50
PANCAKES	1.50

LUNCH

CHEESE SANDWICH	1.50
TUNA SANDWICH	1.50
JELLY SANDWICH	1.50

DINNER

MACARONI AND CHEESE	2.00
BEANS	2.00
HAMBURGER	2.50

ORDER PADS

Cut out square pieces of paper, all the same size. Using felt tip pen, write the name of your restaurant at the top of each piece, and the word "total" at the bottom of each piece. Stack the pieces of paper on top of each other with the name at the top. Using rubber cement, glue the top edge of the stack of paper, as shown. (You may have to glue the edge several times.) Now you have a pad of paper to take orders on!

MONEY

Use the instructions from page 42 to make the money for your restaurant.

PLACE MATS

Place mats are made of construction
paper, then decorated with designs
of different colored construction
paper and felt tip pens.

A BIRTHDAY PARTY

To make a fun birthday party, make a list of all the things you will need. Also decide on a theme and one or two colors that will be used on all the items to make them go together.

1. Birthday Party Poster
2. Name Tags
3. Birthday Card
4. Invitations
5. Game
6. Party Hats
7. Decorations

BIRTHDAY PARTY POSTER

See instructions for a birthday party poster on page 27.

NAME TAGS

To make the name tags, cut small squares out of construction paper, then carefully write each persons name on a separate square with light pencil. Ink or paint over the names, then erase the pencil lines when dry. You can decorate the name tags with paint or pieces of bright colored construction paper.

BIRTHDAY CARD

1. Decide what your birthday card should look like and what it should say. Draw some rough layouts on scrap paper. Use the same colors you are using for your birthday party.
2. Pick the layout you like best.
3. Cut the card out of colorful construction paper, then fold in half.
4. Measure the space for the words on the outside of the card, and draw in light pencil lines. Then, draw each letter carefully, starting with the middle letter.
5. Carefully go over your letters with paint or felt tip pen. Erase pencil lines after the ink or paint is dry.
6. Add some festive decorations with paint, felt tip pens or construction paper

50.

BIRTHDAY GAME

This is a game similar to "pin the tail on the donkey," but we made "pin the nose on the clown" instead.

Draw the parts of the clown on different colors of construction paper, these are simple shapes (see example). Cut out the parts, then glue the pieces onto a large piece of construction paper. Cut out lots of clown noses. Do not glue the noses on the clown! Now you can use push pins to play "pin the nose on the clown" (but be careful!).

53.

PARTY HATS

Fold a large piece of construction paper in half.
Cut paper into a triangle, from corner to corner.
Glue the open edges together. Add decorations
by cutting out different colored shapes of paper
and gluing them on the hat. You can also paint
your hat if you want to. Cut crepe paper into 1/2"
strips and glue on the top of the hat. You can make
hats for everybody, or it might be fun to have them
make their own!

DECORATIONS

You can make all kinds of decorations for your party. You can make banners, streamers and fun signs. Use your imagination!

4
BASIC FOOD GROUPS

GRAINS AND CEREALS

FRUITS AND VEGETABLES

BUTTER

DAIRY PRODUCTS

JAMIE FOR PRESIDENT

5.

PROJECTS

Now we will use the information we have learned in the previous chapters to make projects for home and school. These can be lots of fun to make and useful too! You may want to ask your teacher at school if you can make a project for extra credit.

You can also use the lettering styles and designs you have learned, along with your imagination, to make up projects of your own. Be creative!

ELECTION POSTER

Make a poster for you or a friend to be elected for a school office.

1. Plan your project carefully. Decide what the poster should say. Use the least amount of words possible to make it easier to read. Draw a rough layout of your poster on a piece of scrap paper.

2. This poster was made with paper letters purchased at an art store.
3. Using a ruler, draw light pencil lines where you want the words to be. Figure out the spacing of the letters and glue them on your poster board.
4. Add some bright colored decorations to help bring attention to your poster.

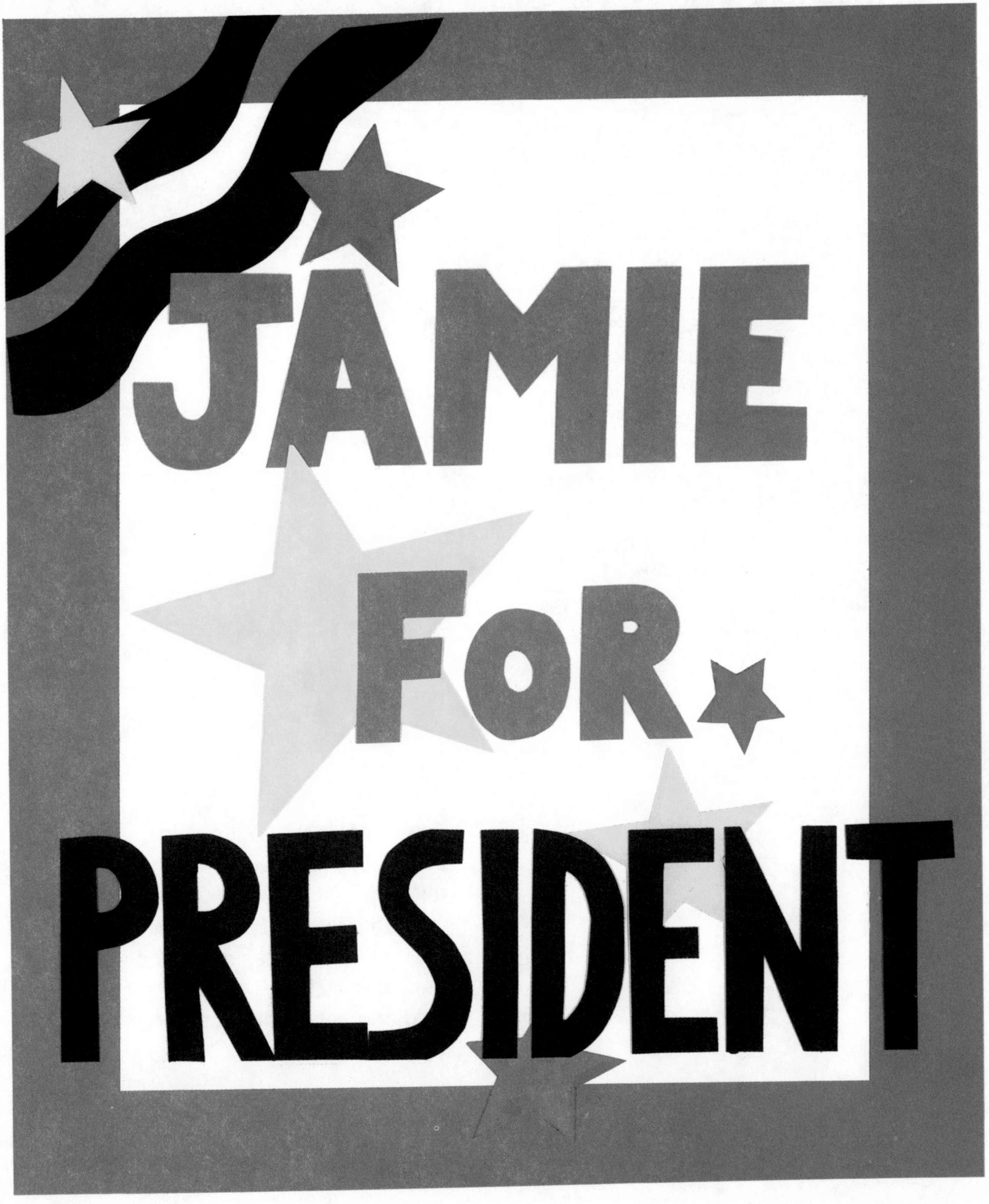
JAMIE
FOR
PRESIDENT

FOOD GROUPS

You can make a poster of the four basic food groups for school. Think of other projects you can make.

1. Plan your project carefully. Decide what the poster should say. Use the least amount of words possible to make it easier to read. Draw a rough layout of your poster on a piece of scrap paper.
2. Draw light pencil lines where you want your words and pictures to go. Draw in the words, then go over the pencil lines with press on letters.
3. Draw the pictures of the four food groups on different colors of construction paper. Use the examples shown here or make up your own.

4. Draw details on your pictures with pencil, then go over the pencil with felt tip pens. Erase the pencil lines when the ink is dry.
5. Cut out the pictures of the food and glue them on your poster board. Add any details or decorations that you want.

4
BASIC FOOD GROUPS

GRAINS AND CEREALS

FRUITS AND VEGETABLES

BUTTER

DAIRY PRODUCTS

MEATS AND OTHER PROTEINS

You can make a collage of almost anything you want. Here is a collage of the United States' first president, George Washington.

1. Plan your project carefully. Decide what the poster or sign should say. Use the least amount of words possible to make it easier to read.
2. Draw a rough layout for your poster on a piece of scrap paper. Decide if you want to add a picture. Try different arrangements and designs.
3. Pick the layout that you like best.
4. Choose the size of letters you will need for the poster. Using a ruler and a pencil, draw parallel lines across your poster the height of your letters apart.

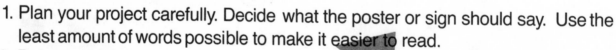

COLLAGE

5. To space your letters, draw the middle letter in the center of the parallel lines with light pencil.
6. Add the rest of the letters, in light pencil, spacing them evenly on either side of the middle letter.
7. Space all of your words this way.
8. Use a felt tip pen to draw over your letters.
9. Erase pencil lines when the ink is dry.
10. Find some photographs or drawings in old magazines or books. You can copy them or cut them out. (Be sure to ask permission first!)

11. You might want to frame your photographs or drawings with construction paper to make your collage more interesting.
12. Glue the pictures on your poster board.

GEORGE WASHINGTON

USA
FIRST
PRESIDENT